Margo R. Friedman, Editor

Glenn C. Mullett, Illustrator

September 11, 2001
God Bless America

To the Children of America, Their Parents, Teachers, and Loved Ones,

During these times of uncertainty, we look to one another for support and comfort. The strength of a great nation rests in the unity of its people. Whatever our heritage, we share a common bond as Americans.

United in purpose, we stand strong. Our spirit soars as we demonstrate to the world we are one—joined at the heart for freedom's sake. As one big family, we courageously march forward with compassion and grace; our collective hands reach out to all nations of peace. May we go forth together with God's blessing.

Perilous times punctuate our American story. From the Revolutionary War to battles of brother against brother, brave men and women fought and died for their beliefs. The passions that stirred our nation's patriots two hundred years ago are the same ones that burn in the souls of our country's leaders today.

Within these pages you will hear the resounding voices of inspirational thinkers, daring philosophers, authors, political leaders, composers, and more. Their words and music still ring true.

Each page is perforated so that the quotes can be easily detached and shared with others. **Patriotism is contagious. May all of you catch it!**

Margo R. Friedman
Mother, Businesswoman, & Former Teacher

Great Ways to Share Patriotism, Exchange Ideas and Foster Conversations
For ages 8 to 80

For Parents, Grandparents, Aunts, Uncles, Sisters, Brothers…

Tear out a favorite quote:
- -Tuck into your child's lunchbox, schoolbag or other special place.
- -Include in your next care package to family and friends.
- -Tape to a mirror.
- -Enclose in a letter or greeting card.
- -Post on the refrigerator or put under a cereal bowl or dinner plate.
- -Drop in a briefcase or tape to a car's dashboard.

For Teachers…

-Write a quote a day on the chalkboard. Encourage discussion about its meaning and how it applies today.

-Allow students to pick a favorite quote, study about the author and research, where possible, the quote's origin.

-Ask students to pretend they are the author of a quote and practice a dramatic delivery for the class.

-Let students divide into teams:

   Each team takes a turn reading a quote; the other team identifies the author and occupation.

   For older children:

   Each team identifies the author and occupation; the other team tries to recite the quote(s) from memory.

-Encourage each member of the class to write their own patriotic quote. Why not have a contest?

Share YOUR suggestions online at www.inhopefreedomrings.com. The best ideas will be posted on our website.

A Special Tribute

IN HOPE, FREEDOM RINGS!

Through tears our bonds grow stronger,
America, our home.
So many lost, so many wronged,
America, our home.

We will go on with firm resolve,
Join hands, together, all.
In honor of our innocent brave,
Join hands, all!

For country and for liberty
One voice we'll raise and sing
As new faith dawns within our land,
In hope, Freedom Rings!

Nancy Moen
Teacher & Poet
September 2001

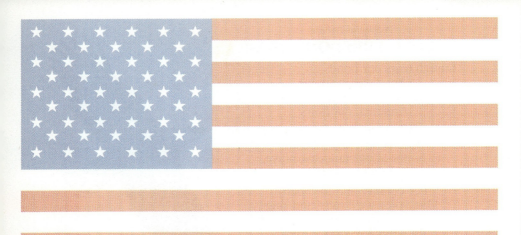

This land is your land, this land is my land,
From California to the New York Island.
From the redwood forest to the Gulf Stream waters,
This land was made for you and me.

Woodrow Wilson (Woody) Guthrie
American Folksinger

...we here highly resolve that the dead
shall not have died in vain; that this nation,
under God, shall have a new birth of freedom,
and that government of the people, by the people,
and for the people, shall not perish from the earth.

Abraham Lincoln
Author of the "Gettysburg Address"
16th President of the United States

I was born an American; I will live an American;
I shall die an American.

Daniel Webster
American Statesman & Orator

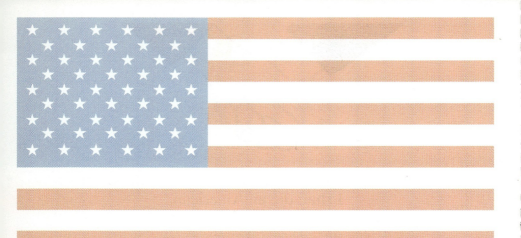

What light is to the eyes–what air is to the lungs–what love is to the heart, liberty is to the soul of man...

Robert G. Ingersoll
American Orator

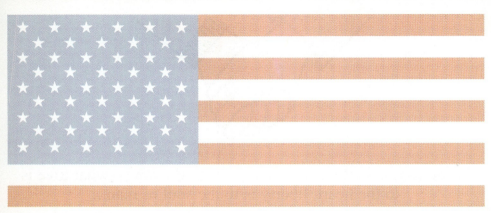

Our nation–this generation–will lift a dark threat of violence from our people and our future. We will rally the world to this cause by our efforts, by our courage.
We will not tire, we will not falter, and we will not fail.

George W. Bush
43rd President of the United States

This massive attack was intended to break our spirit.
It has not done that. It has made us stronger, more
determined, and more resolved.

Rudolph William Giuliani
107th Mayor of New York City

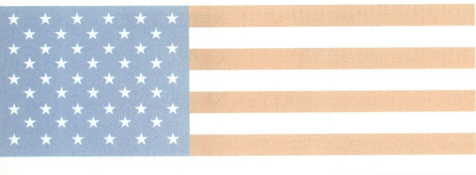

Courage is the price that life exacts
for granting peace with yourself.

Amelia Earhart
American Aviator

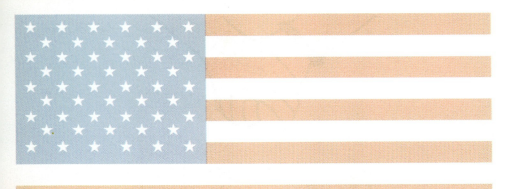

So let me assert my firm belief
that the only thing we have to fear is fear itself.

Franklin D. Roosevelt
32nd President of the United States

Coming together is a beginning;
keeping together is progress;
working together is success.

Henry Ford
American Automobile Manufacturer

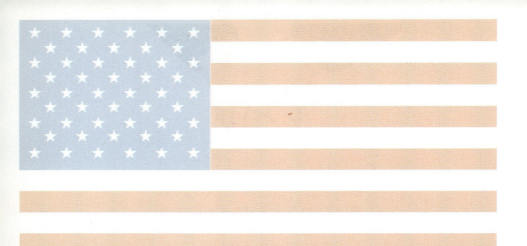

Let every nation know, whether it wishes us well or ill,
that we shall pay any price, bear any burden,
meet any hardship, support any friend, oppose any foe,
in order to assure the survival and the success of liberty.

John F. Kennedy
35th President of the United States

Take time to deliberate;
but when the time for action arrives,
stop thinking and go in.

Andrew Jackson
American General & 7th President of the United States

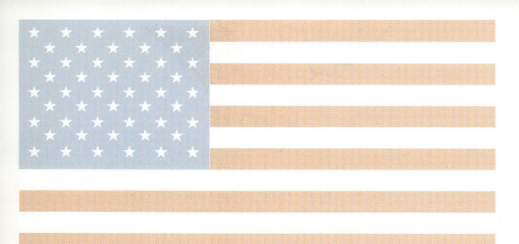

I believe it is the duty of every man to act as though
the fate of the world depends on them.
Surely no one man can do it all.
But, one man CAN make a difference.

Hyman G. Rickover
American Admiral

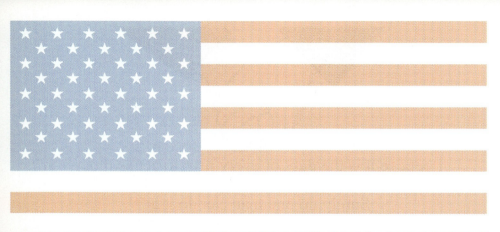

...peace is the highest aspiration of the American People.
We will negotiate for it, sacrifice for it;
we will never surrender for it, now or ever.

Ronald W. Reagan
40th President of the United States

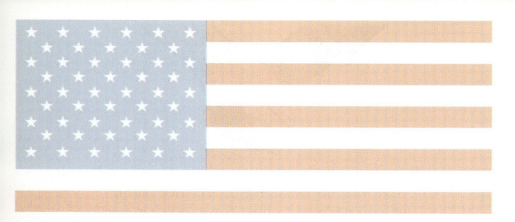

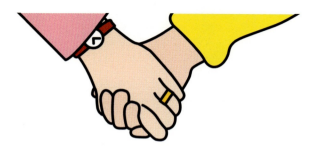

Patience and diligence, like faith, remove mountains.

William Penn
Founder of Pennsylvania

Then conquer we must, when our cause it is just,
And this be our motto—"In God is our trust,"
And the star-spangled banner in triumph shall wave
O'er the land of the free and the home of the brave.

Francis Scott Key
American Lawyer & Author of "The Star-Spangled Banner"

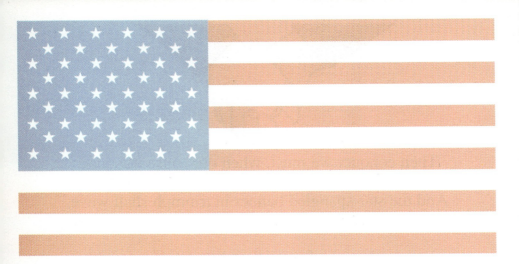

Although the world is full of suffering,
it is full also of the overcoming of it.

Helen Keller
American Lecturer with Blindness & Deafness

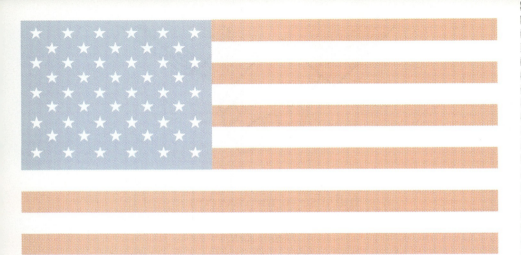

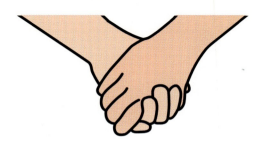

Justice delayed is democracy denied.

Robert F. Kennedy
American Politician & Former U.S. Attorney General

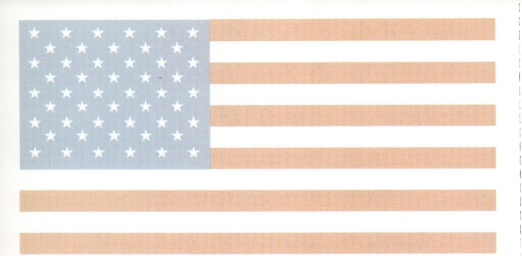

I believe in the sacredness of a promise,
that a man's word should be as good as his bond;
that character–not wealth or power or position–
is of supreme worth.

John D. Rockefeller
American Philanthropist

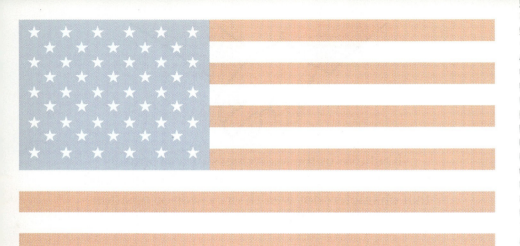

Yet despite the questions we all are asking, regardless of the fears we may be experiencing, one fact is clear:
we will pull together as a nation during this time of crisis.

Jimmy Carter
39th President of the United States & Humanitarian

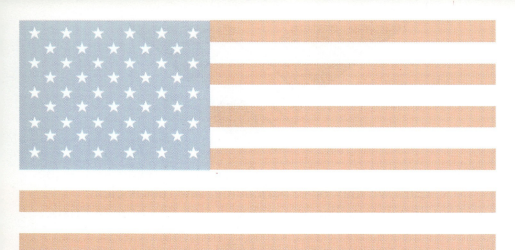

When you cease to make a contribution, you begin to die.

Eleanor Roosevelt
Former First Lady, Humanitarian & Writer

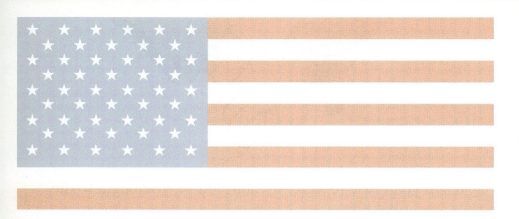

True patriotism is not manifested in short,
frenzied bursts of emotion.
It is the tranquil, steady dedication of a lifetime.

Adlai E. Stevenson
American Politician

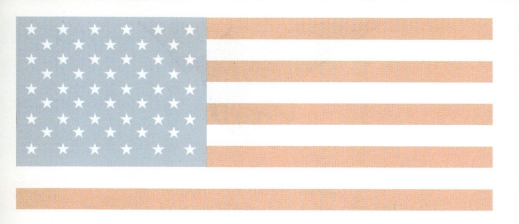

Liberty is a thing of the spirit–to be free to worship,
to think, to hold opinions, and to speak without fear–
free to challenge wrong and oppression with surety of justice.

Herbert Hoover
31st President of the United States

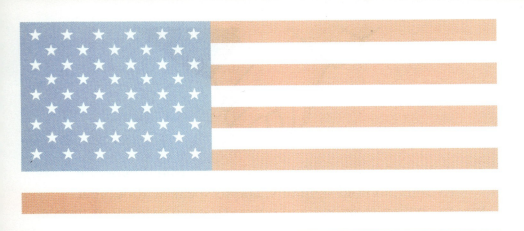

Our flag is red, white and blue, but our nation is a rainbow—
red, yellow, brown, black and white—
and we're all precious in God's sight.

Jesse Jackson
American Clergyman & Political Activist

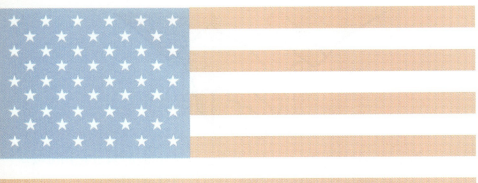

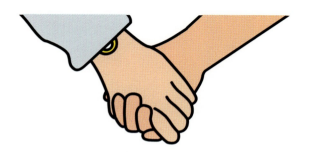

Responding to challenge
is one of democracy's greatest strengths.

Neil A. Armstrong
American Astronaut

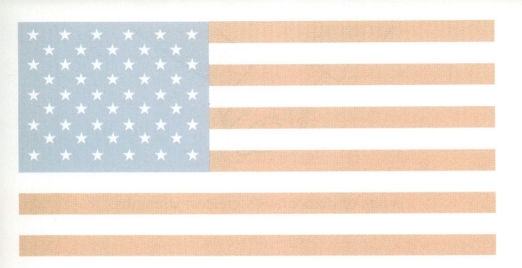

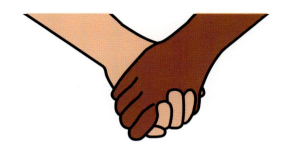

Patriotism is easy to understand in America.
It means looking out for yourself
by looking out for your country.

Calvin Coolidge
30th President of the United States

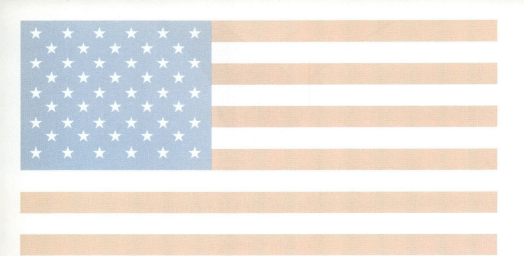

Every calling is great when greatly pursued.

Oliver Wendell Holmes, Jr.
American Jurist

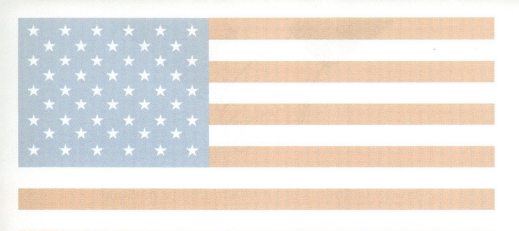

I have never advocated war except as a means of peace.

Ulysses S. Grant
American General & 18th President of the United States

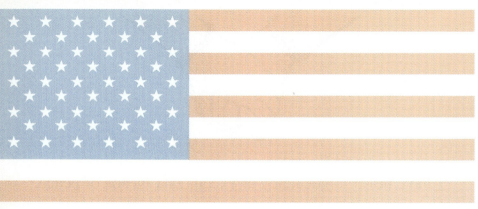

Those who expect to reap the blessings of freedom, must,
like men, undergo the fatigues of supporting it.

Thomas Paine
American Political Philosopher & Author

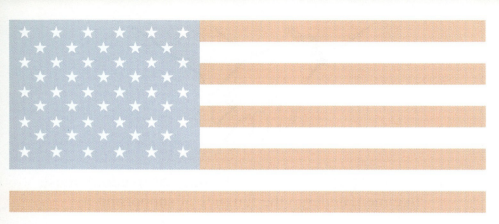

Yours the message cheering
That the time is nearing
Which will see
All men free,
Tyrants disappearing.

"Rock of Ages," A Chanukah Hymn

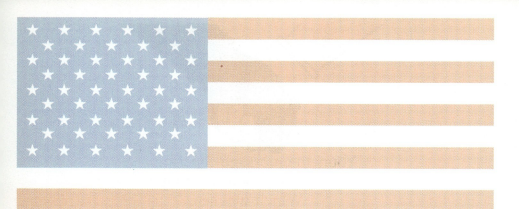

Do what you can, with what you have, where you are.

Theodore Roosevelt
26th President of the United States

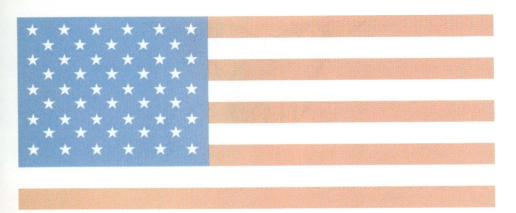

When you get in a tight place and everything goes against you, till it seems you could not hold on a minute longer, never give up then, for that is just the place and time that the tide will turn.

Harriet Beecher Stowe
American Author

The things that the flag stands for were created by the experiences of a great people.
Everything that it stands for was written by their lives.
The flag is the embodiment, not of sentiment, but of history.

Woodrow Wilson
28th President of the United States

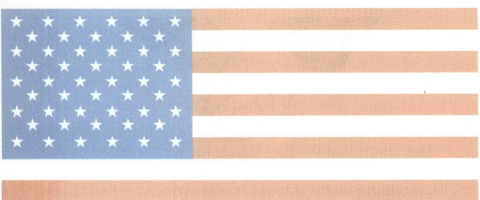

Injustice anywhere is a threat to justice everywhere.

Martin Luther King, Jr.
American Clergyman & Civil Rights Leader

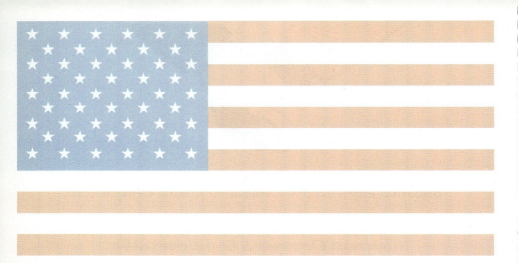

God bless America, land that I love,
Stand beside her and guide her
Through the night with a light from above.
From the mountains, to the prairies,
To the oceans white with foam, God bless America,
My home sweet home.
Irving Berlin
Author of "God Bless America" & American Composer

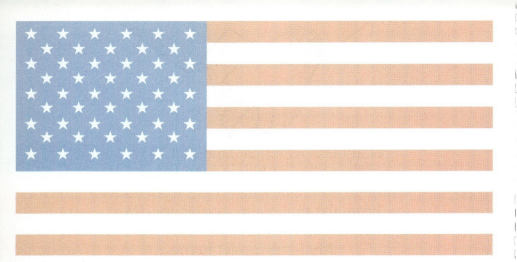

...ask not what your country can do for you–
ask what you can do for your country.

John F. Kennedy
35th President of the United States

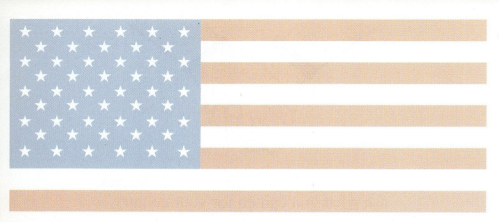

My basic principle is that you don't make decisions because
they are easy; you don't make them because they are cheap;
you don't make them because they are popular;
you make them because they are right.

Theodore Hesburgh
Clergyman & Former President of Notre Dame University

The true test of civilization is—not the census,
not the size of the cities, nor the crops—no,
but the kind of man the country turns out.

Ralph Waldo Emerson
American Essayist & Poet

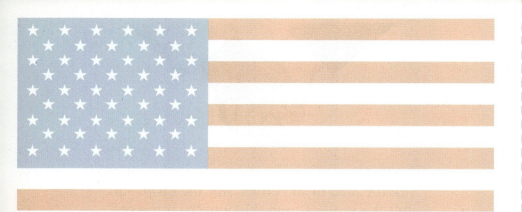

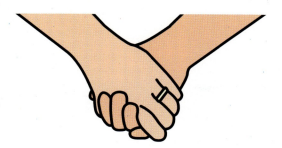

Those who deny freedom to others
deserve it not for themselves, and,
under a just God, cannot long retain it.

Abraham Lincoln
16th President of the United States

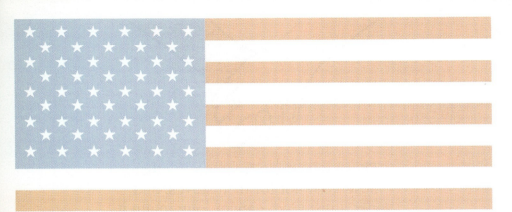

Even if you're on the right track,
you'll get run over if you just sit there.

Will Rogers
American Actor & Humorist

Democracy is a small, hard core of common agreement,
surrounded by a rich variety of individual differences.

James Bryant Conant
American Chemist & Educator

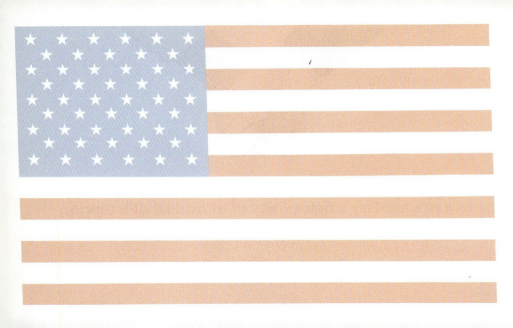

It is an amazing coincidence
that the word American ends in can.

American Saying

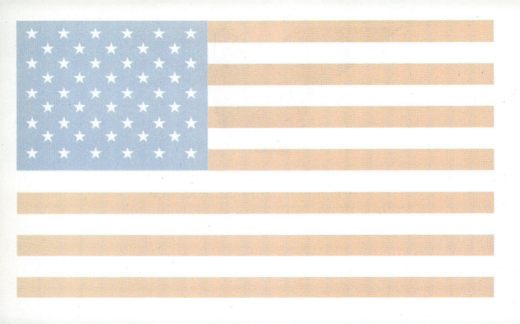

We hold these truths to be self-evident,
that all men are created equal, that they are endowed
by their Creator with certain unalienable Rights, that
among these are Life, Liberty and the pursuit of Happiness...

Thomas Jefferson
Principal Author of the "Declaration of Independence"
3rd President of the United States

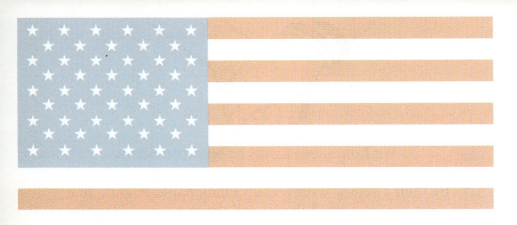

Yesterday is not ours to recover,
but tomorrow is ours to win or lose.

Lyndon B. Johnson
36th President of the United States

We are going to have peace even if we have to fight for it.

Dwight D. Eisenhower
American General & 34th President of the United States

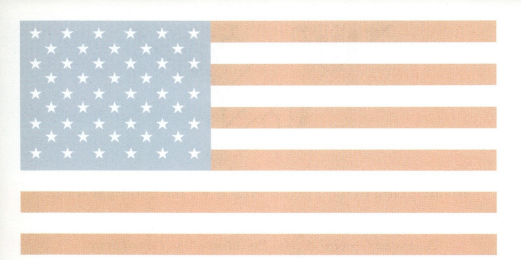

Americans never quit.

Douglas MacArthur
American General

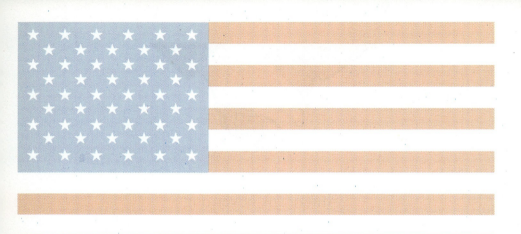

If we as Americans show the same courage and common sense that motivated the men who sat at Philadelphia and gave us the Declaration of Independence and later the Constitution of the United States, there is no domestic problem we cannot solve, and there is no foreign foe we need ever fear.

William F. Knowland
American Politician

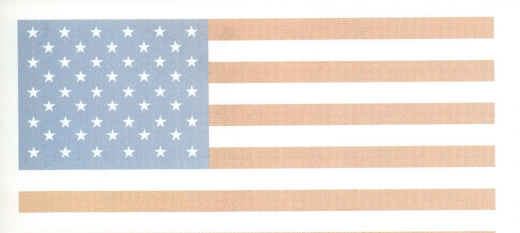

We must always remember that America is a great nation
today not because of what government did for people,
but because of what people did for themselves
and for one another.

Richard M. Nixon
37th President of the United States

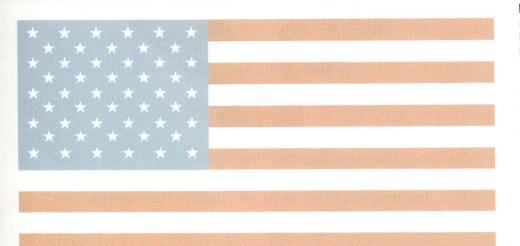

My interest is in the future because I am going to spend the rest of my life there.

Charles F. Kettering
American Electrical Engineer & Inventor

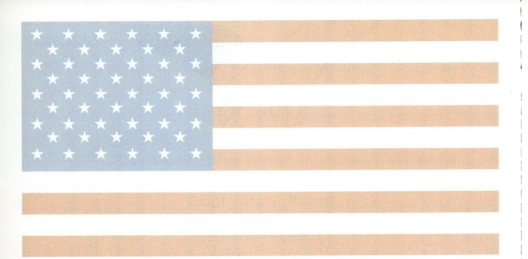

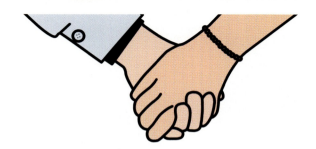

Character, not the circumstances, make the man.

Booker T. Washington
American Educator

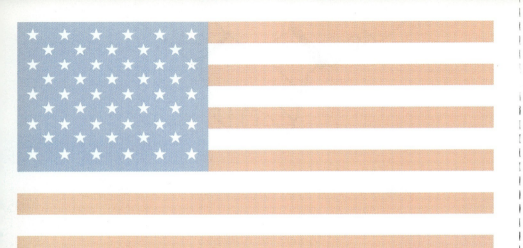

History and destiny
have made America the leader of the world
that would be free.

Colin Powell
American General & Secretary of State

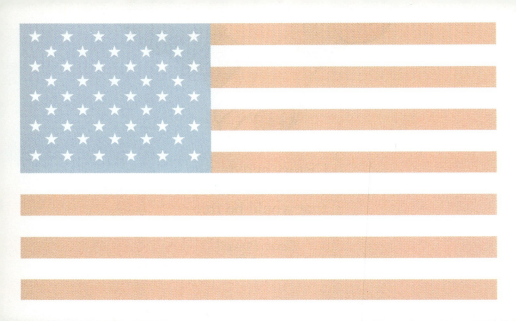

I only regret that I have but one life to lose for my country.

Nathan Hale
American Revolutionary Hero

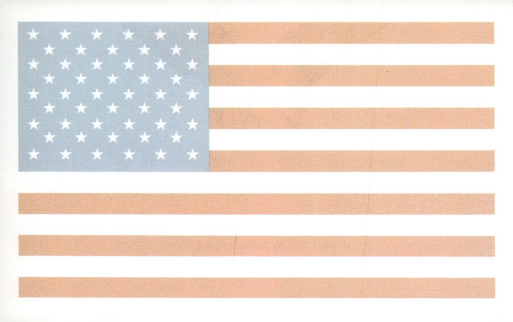

Make no little plans; they have no magic to stir men's blood...make big plans; aim high in hope and work.

Daniel Burnham
American Architect & City Planner

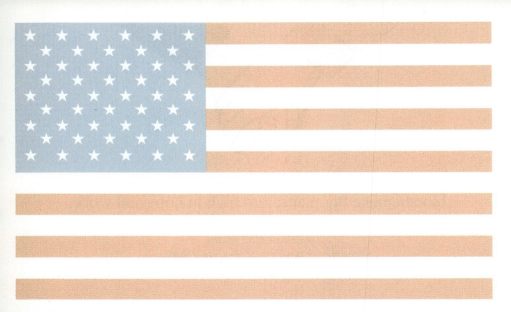

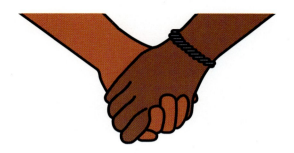

We must all hang together,
or assuredly we shall hang separately.

Benjamin Franklin
American Statesman & Philosopher

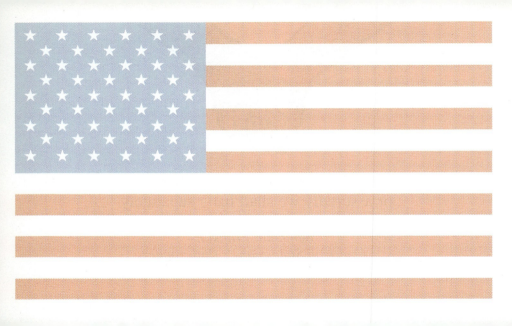

Courage–fear that has said its prayers.

Dorothy Bernard
American Author

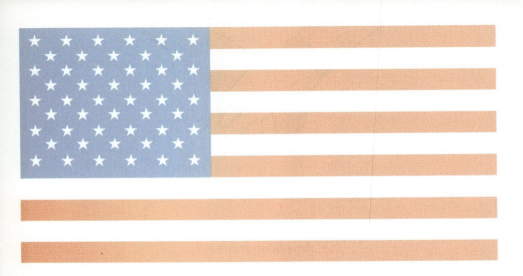

The real democratic American idea is not that every man
shall be on a level with each other,
but that every one shall have liberty,
without hindrance, to be what God made him.

Henry Ward Beecher
American Clergyman

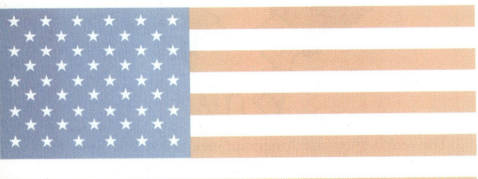

Posterity!
You will never know how much
it cost the present generation to preserve your freedom.
I hope you will make good use of it.

John Quincy Adams
6th President of the United States

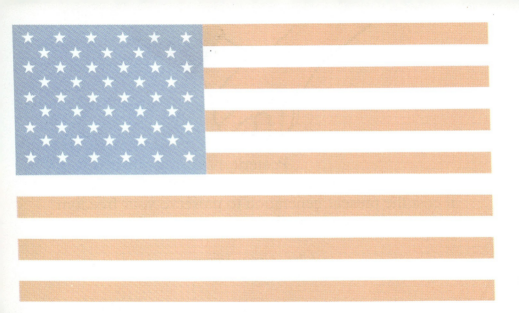

The future depends entirely on
what each of us does every day.

Gloria Steinem
American Author & Feminist

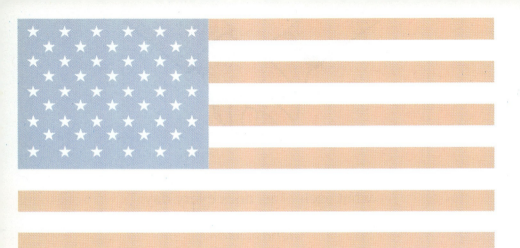

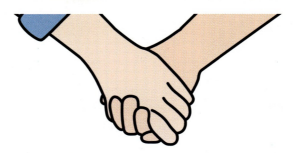

The great thing in this world is not so much where we stand,
as in what direction we are moving.

Oliver Wendell Holmes
American Physician & Author

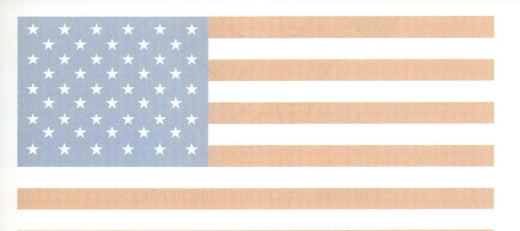

These are the times that try men's souls.

Thomas Paine
American Political Philosopher & Author

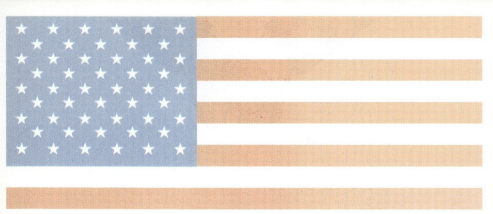

People are afraid of the future, of the unknown.
If a man faces up to it, and takes the dare of the future,
he can have some control over his destiny.

John H. Glenn, Jr.
American Astronaut & Politician

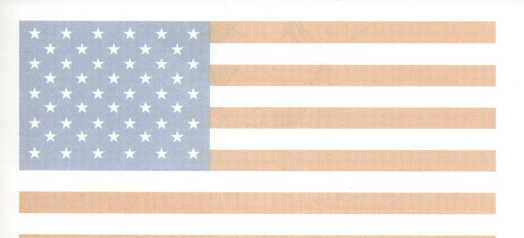

In war or in peace, the naked fact remains the same.
We are given one life; we have one span to live it.
We can wait for circumstances to make
up our minds, or we can decide to act, and in acting, live.

Omar Bradley
American General

Freedom is baffling:
men having it often,
know not they have it,
'til it is gone, and they no longer have it.

Carl Sandburg
American Author & Poet

The future comes one day at a time.

Dean Acheson
American Statesman & Former Secretary of State

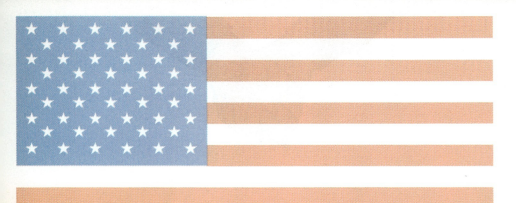

To be prepared for war
is one of the most effectual means of preserving peace.

George Washington
American General & 1st President of the United States

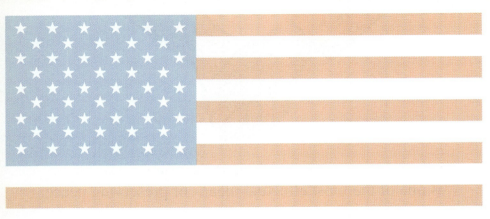

Courage is resistance to fear,
mastery of fear, not absence of fear.

Mark Twain (pen name)
Samuel Langhorne Clemens, American Writer

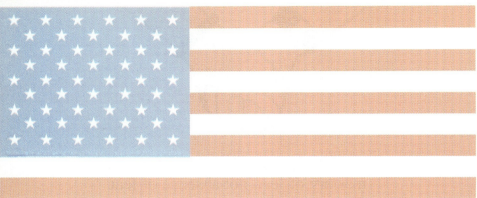

Then join hand in hand, brave Americans all–
by uniting we stand, by dividing we fall.

John Dickinson
American Statesman

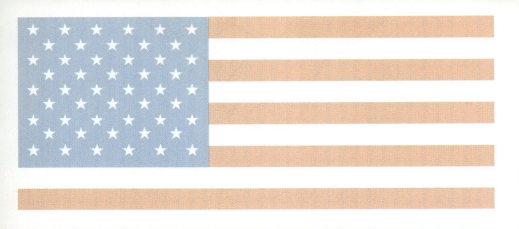

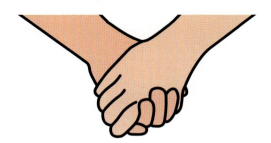

The lesson which wars and depressions have taught is that if
we want peace, prosperity and happiness at home,
we must help to establish them abroad.

Hugo L. Black
American Jurist & Politician

I know not what course others may take; but as for me,
give me liberty, or give me death!

Patrick Henry
American Statesman & Orator

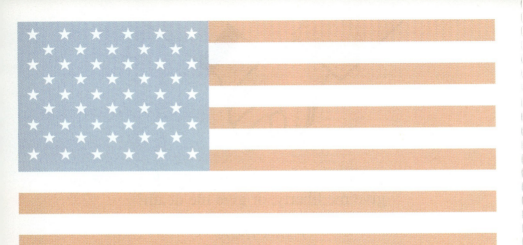

Man's capacity for justice makes democracy possible, but man's inclination to injustice makes democracy necessary.

Reinhold Niebuhr
American Clergyman & Theologian

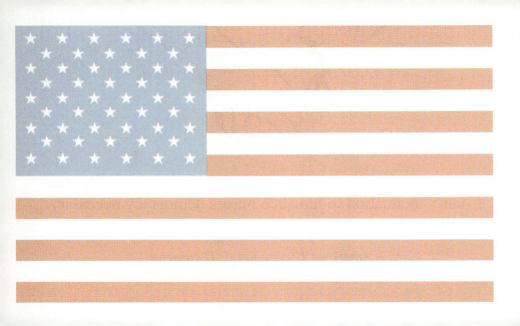

We must build a new world,
a far better world–one in which the
eternal dignity of man is respected.

Harry S. Truman
33rd President of the United States

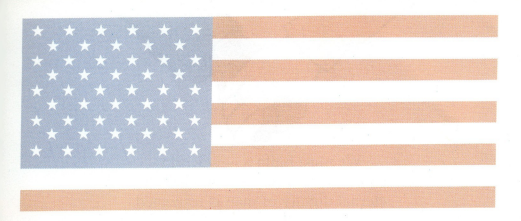

A splendid storehouse of integrity and freedom
has been bequeathed to us by our forefathers.
In this day of confusion, of peril to liberty, our high duty is to
see that this storehouse is not robbed of its contents.

Herbert Hoover
31st President of the United States

The people are the only sure reliance
for the preservation of our liberty.

Thomas Jefferson
3rd President of the United States

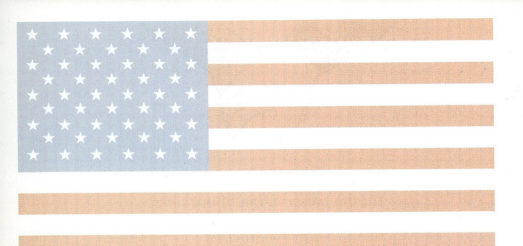

One voice is tiny, and alone it cannot be heard
above the din of politics as usual.
The people's voice, when it cries as one, is a great roar.

Ross Perot
American Businessman & Former Presidential Candidate

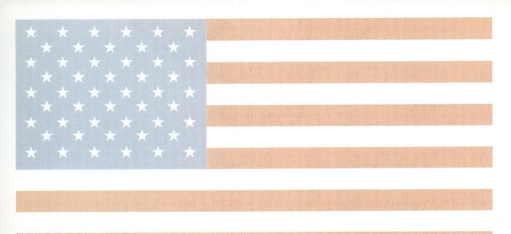

In truth, courage is not at all about emotions.
It is not about how you feel.
It is about how you act.

William J. Bennett
Former Secretary of Education & Author

Liberty is the only thing you cannot have unless you are willing to give it to others.

William A. White
American Journalist

A great nation cannot abandon its responsibilities.
Responsibilities abandoned today
return as more acute crises tomorrow.

Gerald Ford
38th President of the United States

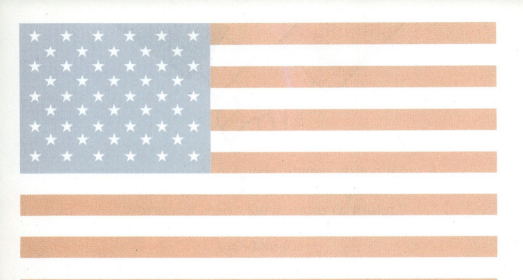

Sometimes it's better to rise up out of the ashes, singing.

Jane Yolen
American Author & Poet

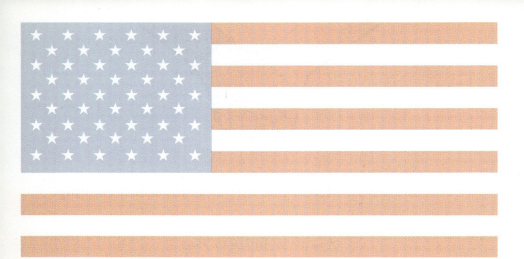

There can be no fifty-fifty Americanism in this country.
There is room here for only a hundred percent Americanism.

Theodore Roosevelt
26th President of the United States

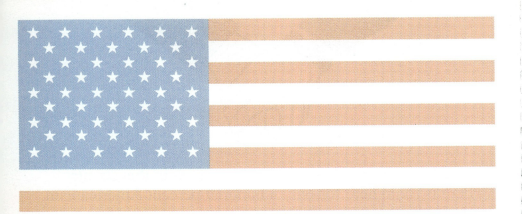

Our grief has turned to anger, and anger to resolution.
Whether we bring our enemies to justice,
or bring justice to our enemies, justice will be done.

George W. Bush
43rd President of the United States

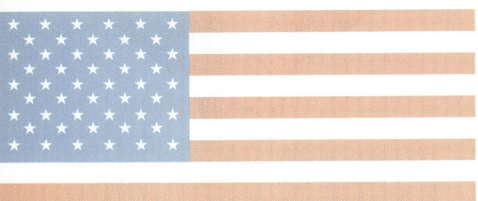

Liberty is its own reward.

Woodrow Wilson
28th President of the United States

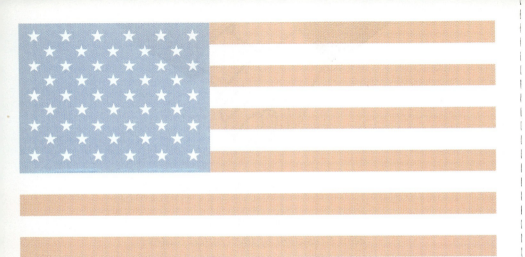

Never before have we had so little
time in which to do so much.

Franklin D. Roosevelt
32nd President of the United States

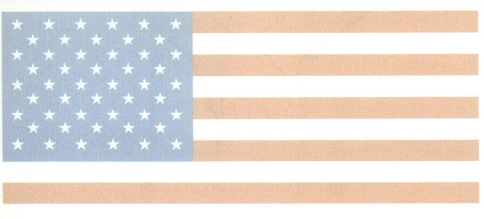

There is no force so democratic as the force of an ideal.

Calvin Coolidge
30th President of the United States

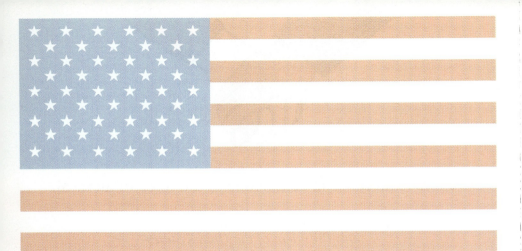

We must learn to live together as brothers
or perish together as fools.

Martin Luther King, Jr.
American Clergyman & Civil Rights Leader

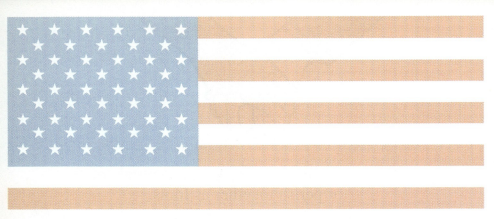

Freedom lies in being bold.

Robert Frost
American Poet

Each generation of Americans must define
what it means to be an American.

William Jefferson Clinton
42nd President of the United States

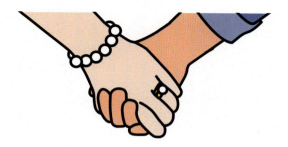

It is a worthy thing to fight for one's freedom; it is another sight finer to fight for another man's.

Mark Twain (pen name)
Samuel Langhorne Clemens, American Writer

If there is righteousness in the heart, there will be beauty in the character. If there is beauty in the character, there will be harmony in the home. If there is harmony in the home, there will be order in the nation. When there is order in the nation, there will be peace in the world.

Chinese Proverb

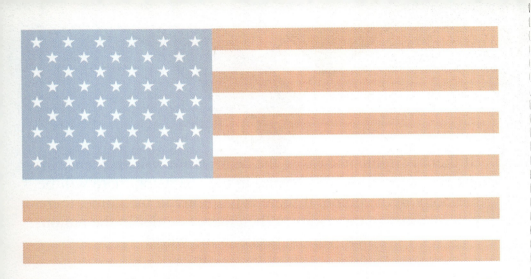

The old ideas are new again because they are not old,
they are timeless: duty, sacrifice, commitment,
and a patriotism that finds its expression
in taking part and pitching in.

George Bush
41st President of the United States

America! America!
God shed His grace on thee!
And crown thy good with brotherhood
From sea to shining sea!

Katharine Lee Bates
American Poet & Author of "America the Beautiful"

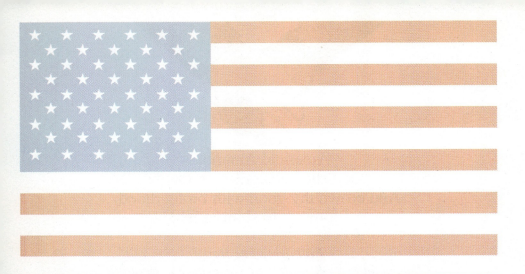

The happy ending is our national belief.

Mary McCarthy
American Writer

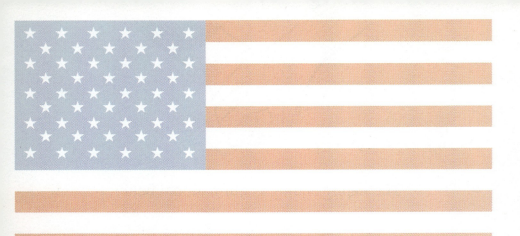

Give me your tired, your poor,
Your huddled masses
yearning to breathe free,
The wretched refuse of
your teeming shore,
Send these, the homeless,
tempest-tossed to me,
I lift my lamp beside the golden door!

Emma Lazarus
(inscription on the Statue of Liberty)
American Author & Poet

Try your own hand at a quote!

_____

_____

_____

_____

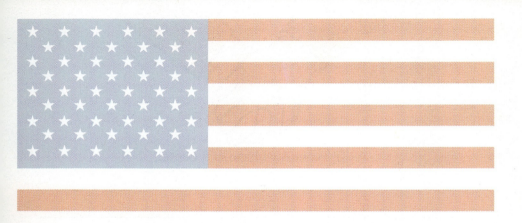

Try your own hand at a quote!

_____

_____

_____

_____